Step by Step

Book Four

Piano Course

by

Edna Mae Burnam

To my students

The exclusive *Playback+* feature allows tempo changes without altering the pitch.
Loop points can also be set for repetition of tricky measures.

To access audio, visit:
www.halleonard.com/mylibrary

Enter Code
3716-0553-4370-2954

ISBN 978-1-4234-3608-9

WILLIS MUSIC

EXCLUSIVELY DISTRIBUTED BY

7777 W. BLUEMOUND RD. P.O. BOX 13819 MILWAUKEE, WI 53213

Visit Hal Leonard Online at
www.halleonard.com

TO THE TEACHER

This is BOOK FOUR of EDNA MAE BURNAM'S PIANO COURSE—STEP BY STEP.

It is designed to follow her BOOK THREE by showing new subjects in logical order and, **one at a time.**

Sufficient work is given on each so that the student will thoroughly comprehend it before going on to the next step.

Besides the music that the student will learn to play and the musical terms that are simply explained, BOOK FOUR, like BOOKS ONE, TWO and THREE, contains written work games. A final check-up may be given by the teacher when the book is finished to assure complete understanding of all work covered.

When the student completes BOOK FOUR the following will have been learned:—

    1.   To be able to name and play the following notes:—

    2.   Read and play in the following key signatures:—

            C Major   F Major

            G Major   B-Flat Major

            D Major

TO THE TEACHER

3. The phrasing of music.
4. The observing and playing of two-note; three-note; and five-note slurs.
5. To count and play triplets.
6. To observe and play D.C. al Fine.
7. To observe and play D.S. al Fine.
8. The meaning and correct pronunciation of the following musical terms and signs:—

WORDS	SIGNS
ALLEGRETTO	*D.C. al Fine*
ANDANTE	*D.S. al Fine* and 𝄋
CRESCENDO	*mp*
DOLCE	*p*
FINE	*pp*
LEGATO	*mf*
MARCATO	*f*
MODERATO	*ff*
PHRASE	>
RITARD.	⌢
SLUR	
SYNCOPATION	
TRIPLETS	
	𝄴

COVERED WAGON DAYS

Notice the word **MODERATO** at the beginning of this piece.

It means to play **moderately fast.**

There is a listing of **expression marks** and their **meanings** on page **52.**

THE PHRASE

A **phrase** is a **musical sentence.**

A phrase is a curved line that looks like this ⌒ and it is placed above the notes that are within it.

Phrases may be either long or short.

This phrase is four measures long.

Here are two short phrases.

Each phrase is two measures long.

When the melody is in the **bass** the phrase mark may be marked thusly:—

Here are two short phrases in the bass.

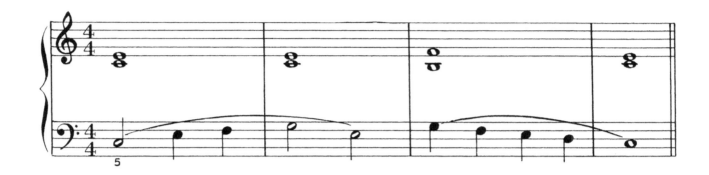

There are four phrases in the following piece.

Notice the **expression** marks.

Each phrase is to be played with different expression.

SPRING FLOWERS

In the following piece, there are two phrases in the **treble** and two phrases in the **bass.**

QUESTIONS AND ANSWERS

TWO NEW C's—LEGER LINE NOTES

A **leger line** is a **short line** made **above** or **below** the staff for notes that are too high or too low to be written on the staff.

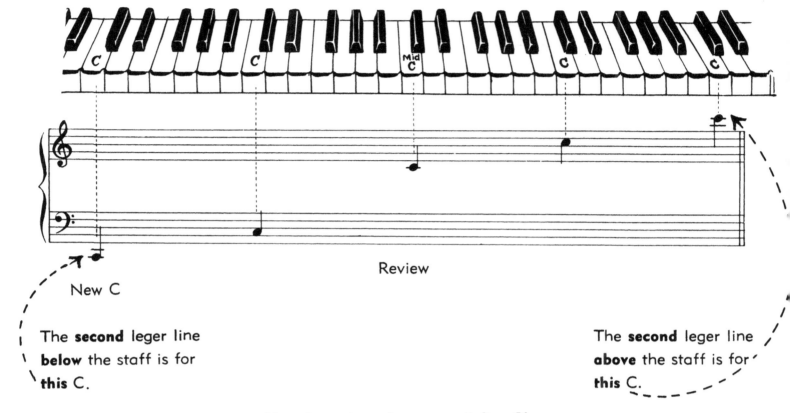

Review

New C

The **second** leger line **below** the staff is for **this** C.

The **second** leger line **above** the staff is for **this** C.

Here is a piece that uses all five C's.

ELEVATORS

Moderato

mf El - e - va - tors go up high! To the floors up near the sky.

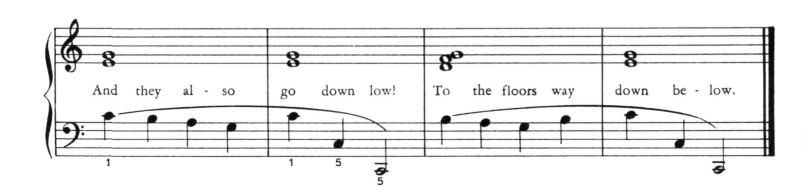

And they al - so go down low! To the floors way down be - low.

THE SLUR

The **slur** is a **curved line** that looks like this 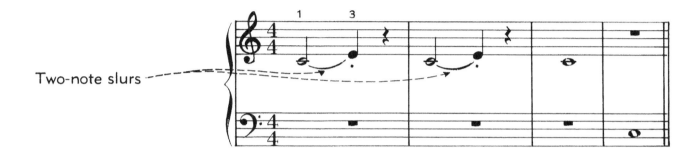 or this either **above** or **below** the notes within it.

A slur consists of two or more notes that should be played **smoothly.**

Your teacher will show you how to play the slurs that are in the following pieces.

Two-note slurs

Three-note slurs

Five-note slurs

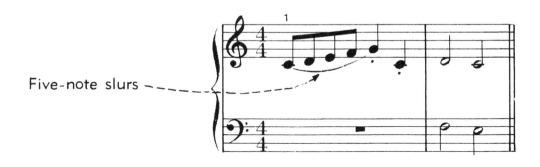

MEXICAN JUMPING BEANS

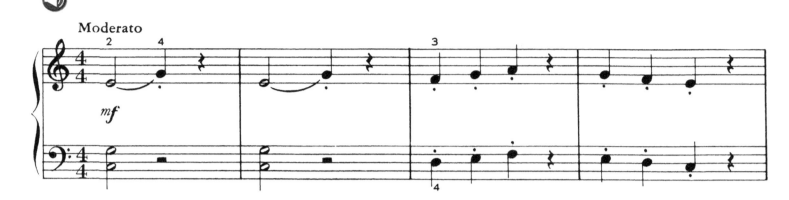

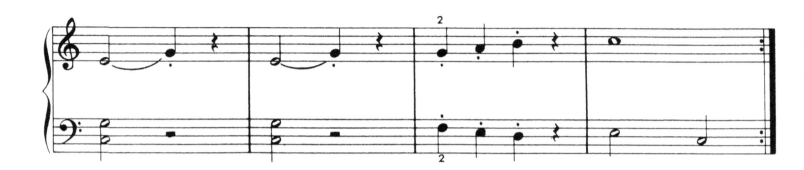

GRANDMOTHER'S TURKEY

Notice the word **ALLEGRETTO** at the beginning of this piece. It means to play **lightly** and **lively**.

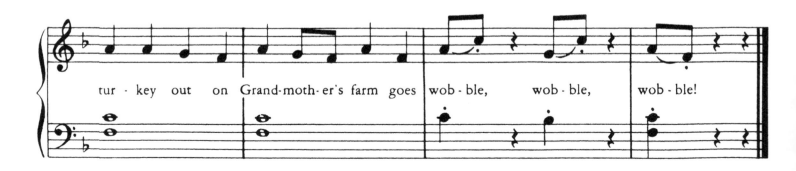

Notice the key signature at the beginning of this piece. This is the key of **D Major.**

The two sharps to remember are **F** and **C.**

Also notice the key signature at the beginning of the **third line.**
This part of the piece is in **G Major.** Remember to sharp every F.

LAVENDER'S BLUE

Arranged by E. M. Burnam

TWINKLE, TWINKLE, LITTLE STAR

Moderato

Arranged by E. M. Burnam

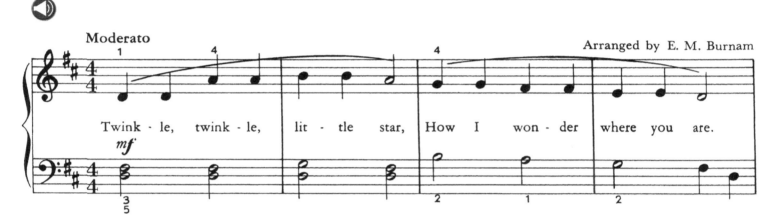

Twink - le, twink - le, lit - tle star, How I won - der where you are.

mf

Up a - bove the world so high, Like a diam - ond in the sky.

Twink - le, twink - le, lit - tle star, How I won - der where you are.

rit.

ANDANTE

Notice the word **ANDANTE** at the beginning of this piece.

It means to play **slowly.**

SANDMAN'S SONG

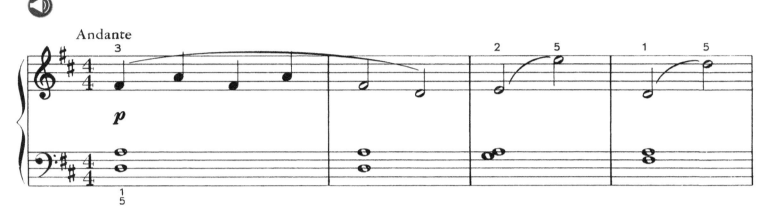

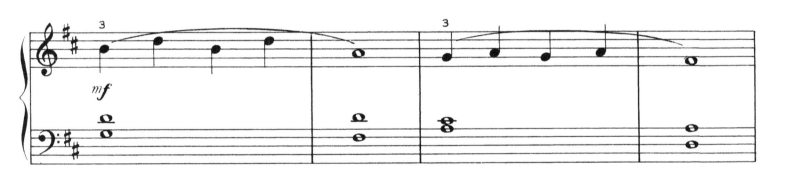

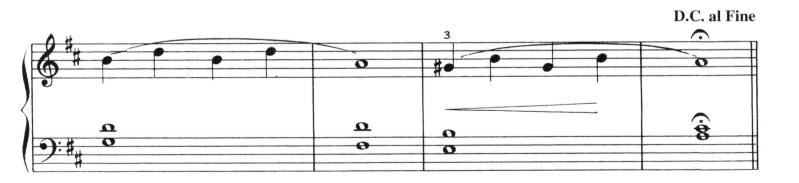

A NEW G

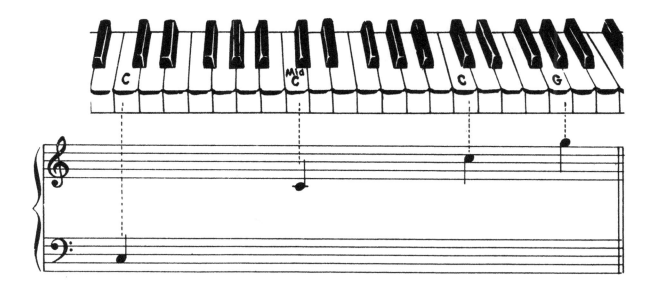

STORYBOOK WALTZ

See the word **LEGATO?** It means to play **smoothly.**

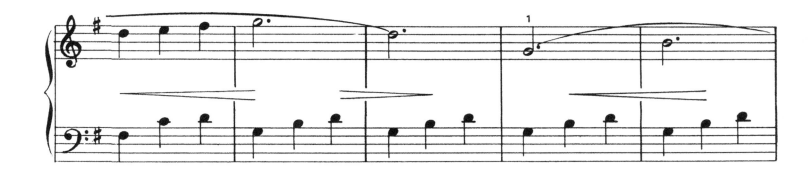

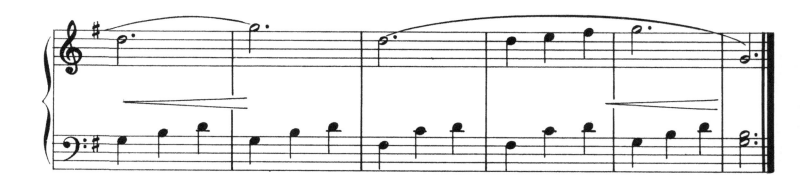

Cresc. — stands for **CRESCENDO.** It means to play **gradually** louder.

CLUNIE, THE CLOWN

Here is an Indian village.

Put the correct sign on each wigwam.

There is a treble clef on the Chief's wigwam—number 1.

Put a **sharp** sign on wigwam   2

Put a **flat** sign on wigwam   3

Put a **natural** sign on wigwam   4

Put a **bass clef** sign on wigwam 5

Put a **hold** sign on wigwam   6

Put an **accent** sign on wigwam 7

Put a **staccato** sign on wigwam 8

Put a **whole note** on wigwam   9

Put a **half note** on wigwam   10

Put a **dotted half note** on wigwam 11

Put a **quarter note** on wigwam 12

Put an **eighth note** on wigwam 13

Put a **quarter rest** on wigwam 14

Put an **eighth rest** on wigwam 15

VALENTINE BOXES

How many Valentines are there in each box?

The notes will tell you.

A quarter note gets one count.

Write the number of Valentines in the heart on top of each box.

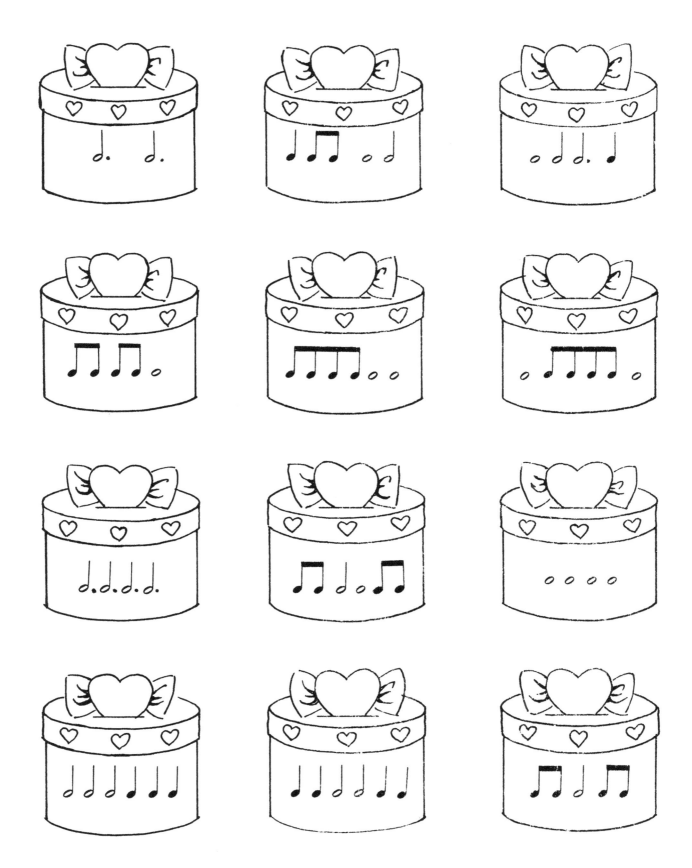

FREIGHT TRAINS

The **treble** train is loaded with sheep.

The **bass** train is loaded with horses.

Write the name of each note just above the note.

A NEW LEGER LINE NOTE

REMEMBER—A **leger line** is a short line **above** or **below** the staff for notes that are too high or too low to be written **on** the staff.

The first line **above** the treble staff is for the note **A.**

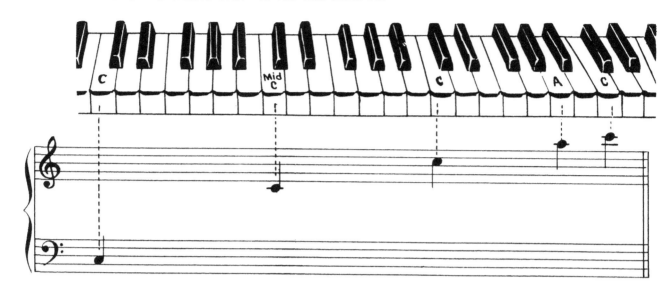

PLAYING IN THE SNOW

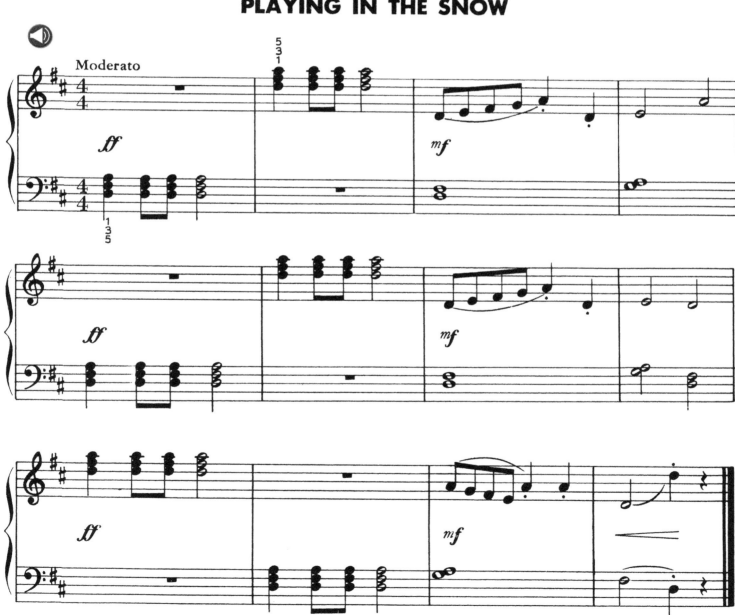

SUNRISE

DOLCE means to play **sweetly** and **softly**.

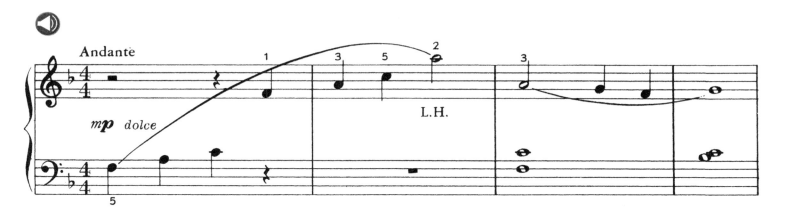

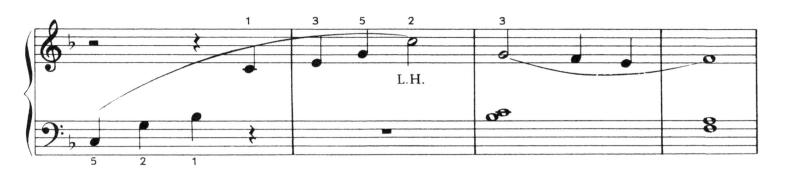

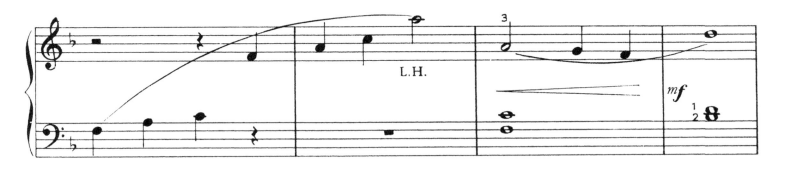

ANOTHER LEGER LINE NOTE

The note just **above** the **first leger line** over the treble staff is **B.**

SPRINGTIME

BALLET DANCER

BRAHMS' "CRADLE SONG"

Arr. by E. M. Burnam

MARCATO

D. S. al Fine is similar to **D. C. al Fine** but differs in one way.

The **S** stands for **"Segno"** (this sign = ✀). It means to **repeat** from **this** sign ✀ and to play to **"Fine"**.

The word **MARCATO** means **marked or accented.**

EVERYBODY MARCH

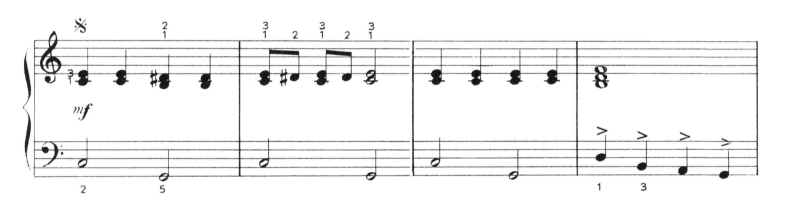

Fine

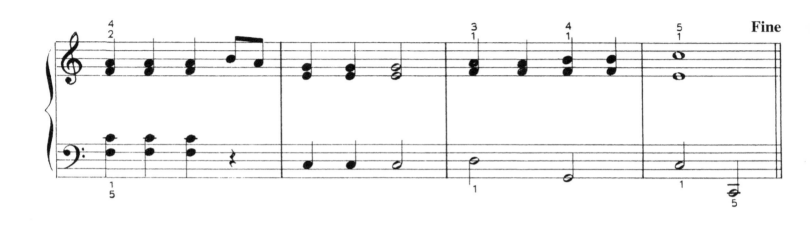

D.S. al Fine

B-FLAT MAJOR

Notice the key signature of the following piece.

It is **B-flat major.**

Remember to **flat** every **B** and **E.**

TULIP TIME IN HOLLAND

TV MARCH

A NEW F

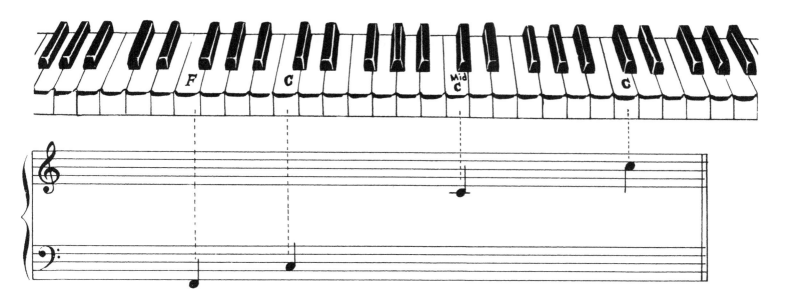

FROM A HOTEL WINDOW

Moderato

When I look from the win-dow wide, Down to streets be- low,

When I look from the win-dow wide, Look 'way down so low.

HOUSES

Each house here is locked.

Draw a line from each key to the house that it matches.

How many houses were you able to unlock?

A MUSICAL CHRISTMAS TREE

Decorate this Christmas tree with musical symbols!

Put a **treble clef** in number 1	Put a **sharp** in number 10
Put a **bass clef** in number 2	Put a **flat** in number 11
Put a **whole note** in number 3	Put a **natural** in number 12
Put a **half note** in number 4	Put a **soft sign** in number 13
Put a **quarter note** in number 5	Put a **very soft sign** in number 14
Put an **eighth note** in number 6	Put a **loud sign** in number 15
Put a **hold sign** in number 7	Put a **medium loud sign** in number 16
Put an **accent mark** in number 8	Put a **very loud sign** in number 17
Put a **staccato mark** in number 9	Put a **medium soft sign** in number 18

QUARTETTE

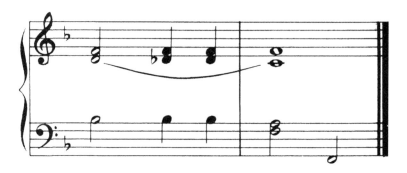

TRIPLETS

When a **group of three notes** have a little **curved line** with the figure **3** — like this  or this
over or under them, this is called a **triplet.**

A **triplet** is a **group** of three notes that get **one count.**

This is an easy way to **count** triplets:—

1 trip-let,   2 trip-let,   3 trip-let

Sing the words as you play this piece.

SONG OF THE TRIPLETS

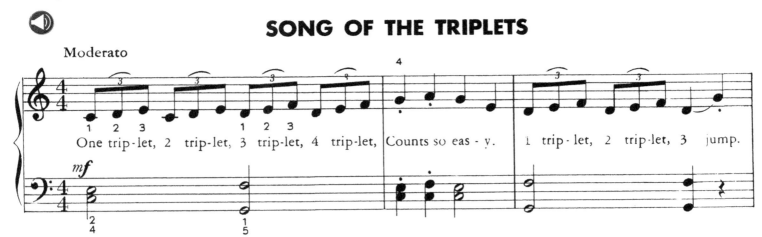

JUANITA

There are some triplets in the **Chorus** of this piece.

Words
Caroline Norton

Spanish Melody
Arr. by E. M. Burnam

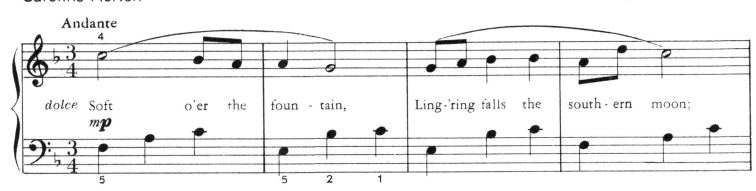

CHORUS

mf Ni - ta, Jua - ni - ta! Ask thy soul if we should part!

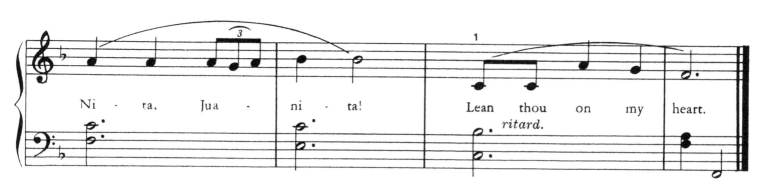

Ni - ta, Jua - ni - ta! Lean thou on my heart. *ritard.*

A NEW LEGER LINE NOTE

The first leger line **below** the **bass staff** is for the note **E**.

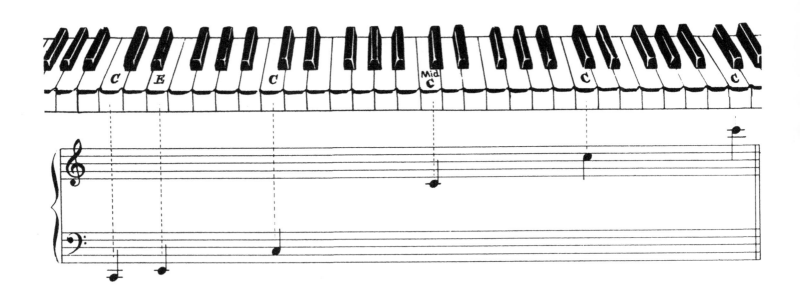

SUBMARINE SAILOR SONG

KEY OF D MAJOR
TRIPLETS

I LIKE TO LOOK AT A RAINBOW

RACING CARS

These cars were in an auto race.

How many times did each car go around the track?

The number of counts in the notes will tell you.

A **quarter** note gets **one** count.

Write the number of times the car went around the track in the space below each car.

RADIOS

Each radio is playing in a different **major key.**

Write the name of the key in the space below each radio.

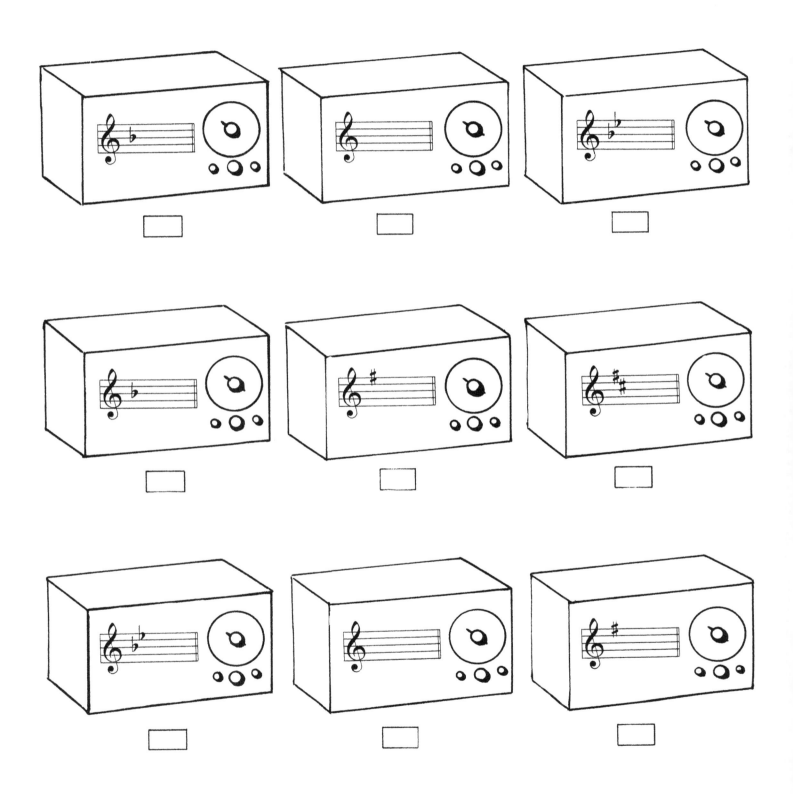

WHISTLING TEAKETTLES

Each teakettle is whistling in a different key.

Write the name of the key in the space between the handle and the kettle.

A NEW LEGER LINE NOTE—D

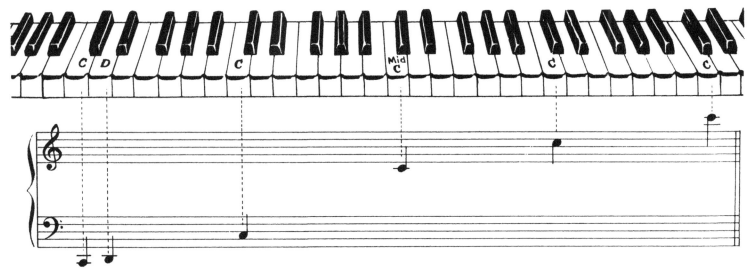

JERRY, THE JUGGLER

SYNCOPATION

SYNCOPATION is a change in the **natural** accent of music.

In most music the **natural accent** is on the **first count** of **every measure,** but there are several measures in the following piece where there is a **strong accent on count "two".** This gives an **unusual rhythmical effect called "syncopation".**

MINSTREL SHOW

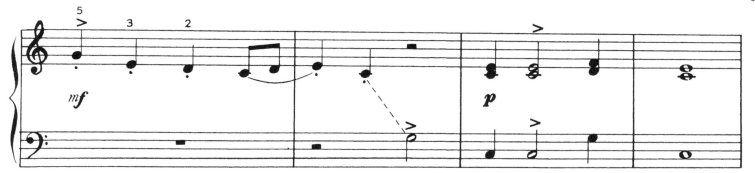

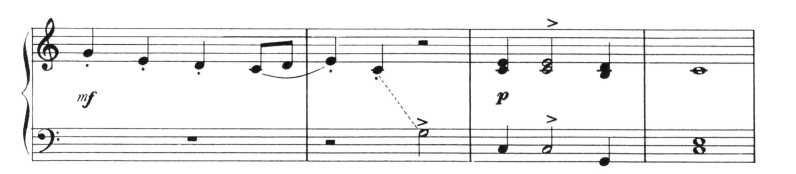

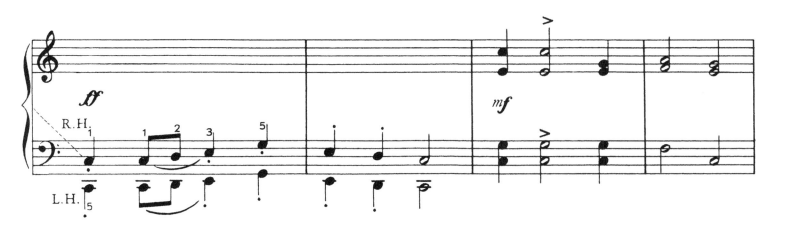

ROCKET TESTING

ANIMATO means with life and spirit.

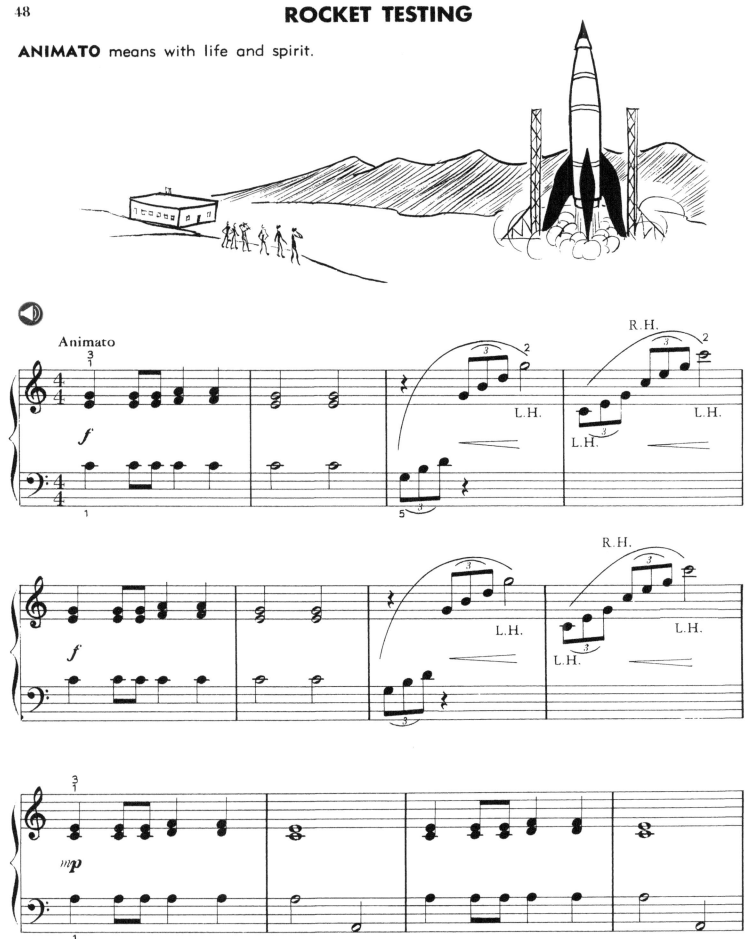

FINAL CHECK-UP

Say aloud the names of the following notes:—

Show me the sign to repeat from when you have **D.S. al Fine.**

Show me a **hold** sign.   >

Show me an **accent** sign.   ⌒
                                                            3

Show me a **staccato** sign.   𝄋

Show me the sign that means **slur.**   .

Show me the sign that means **triplets.**   ⌒

Show me the following key signatures. Also, name the sharps and flats in the key signature in their correct order.

C Major

D Major

G Major

B-Flat Major

F Major

Say aloud and show me the word that means:—

MEANING	WORD
moderately fast	andante
slowly	dolce
softly and sweetly	moderato
light and lively	marcato
gradually louder	ritard.
march time	allegretto
gradually slower	crescendo
smoothly and connected	legato

MUSICAL WORDS AND EXPRESSION MARKS
USED IN THIS BOOK

WORDS

ALLEGRETTO — LIGHT AND LIVELY
ANDANTE — SLOW
ANIMATO — WITH LIFE AND SPIRIT
CRESCENDO — GRADUALLY LOUDER
DOLCE — SWEET
LEGATO — SMOOTH AND CONNECTED
MARCATO — MARKED; ACCENTED
MODERATO — MODERATELY FAST
PHRASE — A MUSICAL SENTENCE
RITARD. — GRADUALLY SLOWER
SLUR — CONNECTED
SYNCOPATION — CHANGE IN NATURAL ACCENT
TRIPLETS — THREE NOTES GET ONE COUNT

SIGNS

\> — ACCENT—EMPHASIS ON NOTE OR CHORD
——— — GRADUALLY LOUDER
——— — GRADUALLY SOFTER
f — LOUD (FORTE)
mf — MODERATELY LOUD (MEZZO FORTE)
ff — VERY LOUD (FORTISSIMO)
p — SOFT (PIANO)
mp — MODERATELY SOFT (MEZZO PIANO)
pp — VERY SOFT (PIANISSIMO)
⌢ — HOLD NOTE OR CHORD LONGER
R.H. — RIGHT HAND
L.H. — LEFT HAND
⌒ — SLUR—CONNECTED
• — STACCATO—SHORT, DETACHED
♩♩♩ — TRIPLET—THREE NOTES GET ONE COUNT
𝄴 — ANOTHER SIGN FOR FOUR-FOUR METER
D.S. al Fine — REPEAT FROM "SEGNO" SIGN 𝄋 AND PLAY TO "FINE"
𝄋 — SEGNO
D.C. al Fine — REPEAT FROM BEGINNING AND PLAY TO "FINE"

Certificate of Merit

This certifies that

....

has successfully completed

BOOK FOUR
OF
EDNA MAE BURNAM'S
PIANO COURSE

STEP BY STEP

and is eligible for promotion to

BOOK FIVE

....Teacher

Date...

Edna Mae Burnam was a pioneer in piano publishing. The creator of the iconic *A Dozen a Day* technique series and *Step by Step* method was born on September 15, 1907 in Sacramento, California. She began lessons with her mother, a piano teacher who drove a horse and buggy daily through the Sutter Buttes mountain range to reach her students. In college Burnam decided that she too enjoyed teaching young children, and majored in elementary education at California State University (then Chico State College) with a minor in music. She spent several years teaching kindergarten in public schools before starting her own piano studio and raising daughters Pat and Peggy. She delighted in composing for her students, and took theory and harmony lessons from her husband David (a music professor and conductor of the Sacramento Symphony in the 1940s).

Burnam began submitting original pieces to publishers in the mid-1930s, and was thrilled when one of them, "The Clock That Stopped," was accepted, even though her remuneration was a mere $20. Undaunted, the industrious composer sent in the first *A Dozen a Day* manuscript to her Willis editor in 1950, complete with stick-figure sketches for each exercise. Her editor loved the simple genius of the playful artwork resembling a musical technique, and so did students and teachers: the book rapidly blossomed into a series of seven and continues to sell millions of copies. In 1959, the first book in the *Step by Step* series was published, with hundreds of individual songs and pieces along the way, often identified by whimsical titles in Burnam's trademark style.

The immense popularity of her books solidified Edna Mae Burnam's place and reputation in music publishing history, yet throughout her lifetime she remained humble and effervescent. "I always left our conversations feeling upbeat and happy," says Kevin Cranley, Willis president. "She could charm the legs off a piano bench," Bob Sylva of the *Sacramento Bee* wrote, "make a melody out of a soap bubble, and a song out of a moon beam."

Burnam died in 2007, a few months shy of her 100th birthday. "Music enriches anybody's life, even if you don't turn out to be musical," she said once in an interview. "I can't imagine being in a house without a piano."

CLASSIC PIANO REPERTOIRE

The *Classic Piano Repertoire* series includes popular as well as lesser-known pieces from a select group of composers out of the Willis piano archives. Every piece has been newly engraved and edited with the aim to preserve each composer's original intent and musical purpose.

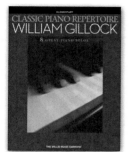

WILLIAM GILLOCK - ELEMENTARY

8 Great Piano Solos

Dance in Ancient Style • Little Flower Girl of Paris • On a Paris Boulevard • Rocking Chair Blues • Sliding in the Snow • Spooky Footsteps • A Stately Sarabande • Stormy Weather.

00416957 ....$8.99

WILLIAM GILLOCK - INTERMEDIATE TO ADVANCED

12 Exquisite Piano Solos

Classic Carnival • Etude in A Major (The Coral Sea) • Etude in E Minor • Etude in G Major (Toboggan Ride) • Festive Piece • A Memory of Vienna • Nocturne • Polynesian Nocturne • Sonatina in Classic Style • Sonatine • Sunset • Valse Etude.

00416912 .... $12.99

EDNA MAE BURNAM - ELEMENTARY

8 Great Piano Solos

The Clock That Stopped • The Friendly Spider • A Haunted House • New Shoes • The Ride of Paul Revere • The Singing Cello • The Singing Mermaid • Two Birds in a Tree.

00110228 ....$8.99

EDNA MAE BURNAM - INTERMEDIATE TO ADVANCED

13 Memorable Piano Solos

Butterfly Time • Echoes of Gypsies • Hawaiian Leis • Jubilee! • Longing for Scotland • Lovely Senorita • The Mighty Amazon River • Rumbling Rumba • The Singing Fountain • Song of the Prairie • Storm in the Night • Tempo Tarantelle • The White Cliffs of Dover.

00110229 .... $12.99

JOHN THOMPSON - ELEMENTARY

9 Great Piano Solos

Captain Kidd • Drowsy Moon • Dutch Dance • Forest Dawn • Humoresque • Southern Shuffle • Tiptoe • Toy Ships • Up in the Air.

00111968 ....$8.99

JOHN THOMPSON - INTERMEDIATE TO ADVANCED

12 Masterful Piano Solos

Andantino (from Concerto in D Minor) • The Coquette • The Faun • The Juggler • Lagoon • Lofty Peaks • Nocturne • Rhapsody Hongroise • Scherzando in G Major • Tango Carioca • Valse Burlesque • Valse Chromatique.

00111969 .... $12.99

LYNN FREEMAN OLSON - EARLY TO LATER ELEMENTARY

14 Great Piano Solos

Caravan • Carillon • Come Out! Come Out! (Wherever You Are) • Halloween Dance • Johnny, Get Your Hair Cut! • Jumping the Hurdles • Monkey on a Stick • Peter the Pumpkin Eater • Pony Running Free • Silent Shadows • The Sunshine Song • Tall Pagoda • Tubas and Trumpets • Winter's Chocolatier.

00294722 ....$9.99

LYNN FREEMAN OLSON - EARLY TO MID-INTERMEDIATE

13 Distinctive Piano Solos

Band Wagon • Brazilian Holiday • Cloud Paintings • Fanfare • The Flying Ship • Heroic Event • In 1492 • Italian Street Singer • Mexican Serenade • Pageant Dance • Rather Blue • Theme and Variations • Whirlwind.

00294720 ....$9.99

WILLIS MUSIC

EXCLUSIVELY DISTRIBUTED BY
HAL•LEONARD®

View sample pages and hear audio excerpts online at **www.halleonard.com**

www.willispianomusic.com

www.facebook.com/willispianomusic

Prices, content, and availability subject to change without notice.